SPORTS FOR FUN AND FITNESS

GYMNASTICS FOR FUN AND FITNESS

Ty Schalter

Enslow Publishing
101 W. 23rd Street
Suite 240
New York, NY 10011
USA
enslow.com

Published in 2020 by Enslow Publishing, LLC.
101 W. 23rd Street, Suite 240, New York, NY 10011

Library of Congress Cataloging-in-Publication Data

Names: Schalter, Ty author.
Title: Gymnastics for fun and fitness / Ty Schalter.
Description: New York : Enslow Publishing, 2020 | Series: Sports for fun and fitness | Audience: K-4. | Includes bibliographical references and index.
Identifiers: LCCN 2019013447| ISBN 9781978513396 (library bound) | ISBN 9781978513372 (paperback) | ISBN 9781978513389 (6 pack)
Subjects: LCSH: Gymnastics--Juvenile literature. | Gymnastics for children--Juvenile literature.
Classification: LCC GV461.3 .S33 2019 | DDC 796.44--dc23
LC record available at https://lccn.loc.gov/2019013447

Printed in the United States of America

To Our Readers: We have done our best to make sure all website addresses in this book were active and appropriate when we went to press. However, the author and the publisher have no control over and assume no liability for the material available on those websites or on any websites they may link to. Any comments or suggestions can be sent by email to customerservice@enslow.com.

Photo Credits: Gymnastics – Research by Bruce Donnola

Cover, p. 1 (gymnastics athletes) Image Source/Getty Images; cover and interior pages (balls and birdie) Lightspring/Shutterstock.com; p. 7 Africa Studio/Shutterstock.com; p. 8 Ezra Shaw/Getty Images; p. 10 David Tadevosian/Shutterstock.com; p. 13 Mihai Blanaru/Shutterstock.com; p. 14 Undrey/Shutterstock.com; p. 16 Michael C. Gray/Shutterstock.com; p. 19 Iakov Filimonov/Shutterstock.com; p. 20 Rawpixel.com/Shutterstock.com; p. 22 Rvector/Shutterstock.com; p. 24 Sasha Samardzija/Shutterstock.com; p. 25 © iStockphoto.com/master1305; p. 27 Mariana Aabb/Shutterstock.com

Contents

Introduction

Human beings can't fly, but gymnasts come pretty close. From vaults and tumbling runs to release skills and dismounts, gymnasts' bodies can do incredible things—and gymnasts support each other, express themselves, and have lots of fun along the way.

If you've watched the Summer Olympics, you've seen gymnasts at their best: Men and women performing feats of strength, skill, balance, flexibility, and **coordination** in each of eight different **events**.

The Olympics, in fact, are where the sport of gymnastics began almost three thousand years ago, in Greece. The original Olympics were a festival celebrating the ancient Greek god Zeus. The Greeks valued physical fitness so much that they held athletic competitions during their festivals as a way to honor their gods. For the Olympic

Games, the biggest and most famous competition, the Greeks would even pause all their wars so that the best athletes from all around could compete!

The word "gymnastics" comes from ancient Greek words meaning exercise and discipline. Today, that's still the foundation of gymnastics. The Olympics remain the most famous competition in the sport.

Olympic-level gymnasts are some of the best athletes in the world. Top-notch strength, speed, and jumping power are required to do the kind of gymnastics skills you see on TV. But that's not all: **flexibility**, balance, and control are no less important for flipping and twisting with perfect form.

Judges score these **routines** based on how hard the skills are and how perfectly they are performed. Each competitor's score is added up for their individual **all-around** total, and teammates' all-around scores combine to make team scores.

But even if you never stand on a **podium** or salute a judge, the sport of gymnastics can help you have fun and get fit. You don't need to be able to jump out of the gym or lift huge weights to get started. You just need you!

CHAPTER 1

Warming Up

Stretching and warming up are important parts of getting ready to do any exercise. By loosening up your muscles and getting your blood flowing, you're more likely to do your best right away—and less likely to get hurt.

In gymnastics, though, stretching and warmups are especially important. Good flexibility can be the difference between just barely doing a skill and doing it really well—like doing a cartwheel with perfectly straight legs instead of bent ones.

Stretching is an important part of gymnastics. It gets your muscles ready for tumbling, jumping, and cartwheels.

Getting Pumped

You don't walk into the gym and start doing gymnastics skills without first getting your muscles loose and heart pumping. If you're on a team getting ready for a **meet**, your coach will tell you exactly what warm-ups

The Olympics is an international sports competition that takes place every four years, but you can practice gymnastics any day!

NOT JUST EVERY FOUR YEARS

Olympic-level gymnastics is amazing and inspiring, but there are always great competitions going on at high schools and colleges around the world. High school meets are lots of fun to watch! They're cheap to attend, and you can come and go as you please. It's a great way to stay inspired—and you might even be able to pick up some tips.

to do, and when to do them, so you'll be just the right amount of ready when competition begins. If you are by yourself, warming up like this will still help you get ready (and get better).

To get your feet ready to bounce, some simple jumps in place (or jump rope, or jumping jacks) do the trick. Then start moving: Walk while raising your knees high, twisting your torso, or swinging your arms extra-high. Break into a jog and do a light run for several minutes. Try mixing in some high-knee strides or skips. Try lifting your feet on the back of each stride so you "kick" yourself in the rear; you'll feel your thighs stretch as you do. Finally, some arm swings, trunk twists, and hip circles will get you ready to do your stretching and conditioning routines.

Stretching Your Limits

Like any athletic skill, flexibility is something you have to get better at little by little over a long time. When stretching, take the stretch to where you feel your muscles

Flexibility is the ability to bend without breaking. The more you practice, the more flexible you can become.

begin to get uncomfortable, then hold it while you slowly count to 20. Keep it up every single day, and soon you'll realize you can stretch more without getting uncomfortable. Eventually you'll be stretching farther and farther, able to hold more perfect forms for longer.

One great way to stretch your legs is the **splits**. To do a beginner split, start on your hands and knees. Then slide your knees farther apart until you feel the stretch in the insides of your upper legs. After lots of practice stretching to your limit and holding, you'll be able to get closer and closer to the ground. Try it with one straight leg, and then both legs straight.

If you have a coach, they'll instruct you on lots of great ways to stretch your legs, ankles, wrists, and more. If you don't have a coach, be sure to check out the books and websites in the "Learn More" section to make sure all your important muscles are getting prepared!

CHAPTER 2

Basic Skills and Conditioning

All warmed up? Okay, you're ready to work on getting better! Basic conditioning will help you build the strength and endurance to do many skills in a row—and eventually, to do a routine.

Conditioning

When we think of building strength, we usually think of big muscles—especially big arm muscles. But strength

A

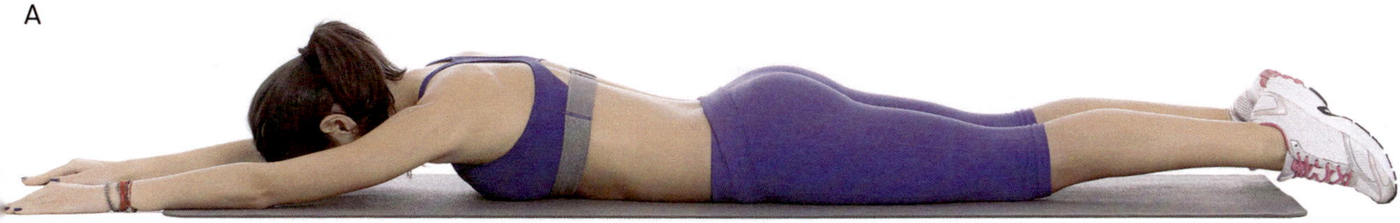

B

To do the Superman exercise, lie on the floor with your arms stretched out. Then lift your arms and legs like you're flying!

starts with your **core**, and working stomach and back muscles is key for gymnastics skills.

Before you start exercises like these, make sure you're properly stretched and warmed up, as instructed by your coach or in Chapter 1.

First, try the seal stretch: Lay flat on your tummy, then use your arms to push just your shoulders off the

It's important to work with a coach, especially when you haven't done a move before. Coaches keep you safe and show you how to improve.

ground. Keep your legs straight and together and your hips on the ground. You should feel the stretching in your stomach and back. Then, you can try stomach exercises like crunches or the **Superman exercise**.

Training to improve your flexibility, strength, agility, and toughness will help you in everything you do—and so will having the dedication to practice skills over and over again until you do them just right every time.

Practice every day, pushing yourself a little bit harder, and you'll discover you've got the energy and ability to do everything better: running, jumping, climbing, playing other sports—and maybe be able to impress your friends with some snappy cartwheels.

Basic Skills

The first skill most gymnasts learn is the forward roll. Squat down with your feet together, and place your hands

SAFETY FIRST!

Important: Work out only in a safe space with a soft floor surface clear of obstacles and other people—ideally, a gymnastics or other workout mat. Never try a skill in a dangerous environment or without adult supervision, especially one you haven't tried before. If you don't have a coach, ask a trusted adult who knows how to do the skill to watch and help you until you and the adult are both confident that you can do it on your own.

Learning how to do a cartwheel is one of the most fun things in gymnastics! It's okay to ask for help as you learn them.

on the ground in front of you. Put your head down on the ground, between your hands. Then straighten your legs, pushing your hips up over your head. Your body will naturally roll from your head to your back. Use your **momentum** to carry you forward; try to put your feet back down and stand up without using your hands!

Another great beginner skill is the cartwheel. Start by standing up straight, with your arms up by your ears.

One leg should be out forward and bent slightly, with the back leg straight (you'll have to figure out which leg feels more comfortable for you).

Reach your hands down and forward together. As you bring your hands down to the ground, turn them so one will be farther away from you. Push hard with your arms, and kick your back leg up and out to the side. Once you get to where you can do this in one smooth motion, momentum will carry your kicking leg over, and your planted leg will follow. You should end up facing opposite the direction you started. You may find it easier to start with a "baby cartwheel," where you don't have to lift your legs high.

As you get better and stronger, try to kick your back leg up straight over your head, and bring the other one straight over as well. You'll feel your torso twist as you do it, and you'll really feel like a rolling wheel!

CHAPTER 3

Finding a Gym

There's only so far you can take your skills without proper equipment and a coach to guide you. Fortunately, there are lots of places you can go to get better!

At School

Most elementary and middle school physical-education classes have a gymnastics unit. They usually cover basic

Gymnastics centers are places where teams and individuals gather to use equipment and share tips about the sport.

stretches and skills like those in this book. They may also have an **apparatus** like a balance beam. This is a good way to get a taste for the sport with proper mats and instruction.

Schools will often have you do your workout in socks to keep the mats clean. But gymnasts don't ever train or compete in socks—they're too slippery!

Balance is an important part of gymnastics, too. When you stand on the balance beam, every part of your body is working hard.

Some elementary or middle schools will also offer gymnastics as an after-school activity, usually taught by a parent or teacher.

Parks & Rec

Many communities have a parks and recreation department that offers affordable classes in different activities and sports, including gymnastics. Often, these coaches were competitive gymnasts themselves, and they may have access to more equipment than in regular school classes. This is an even better way to get in shape and to see if gymnastics is the right sport for you.

Private Gyms

When you're ready to get more serious about gymnastics, you'll want to take classes at a dedicated gym. These gyms will have all the apparatus for boys' and girls' gymnastics, as well as full sets of mats and safety equipment. They'll usually offer competitive tracks and

THE RIGHT FIT

Choosing the right gym is very important! Try to visit several different gyms to get a feel for the coaching, environment, facilities, and commitment level involved. Having coaches you trust and an environment you're excited to come back to is key to loving the sport.

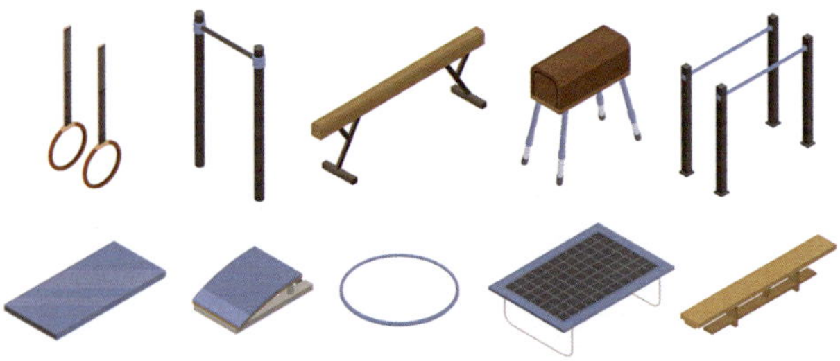

You will use all kinds of equipment in gymnastics, including rings, springboards, uneven bars, and floor mats.

participation in meets as options. This is a more serious time and money commitment, involving practice multiple times a week.

Coaches, especially the senior ones, should have a USA Gymnastics safety certification—this ensures that they not only know how to teach skills well, but also have passed background checks and follow Safe Sport policies.

Some gyms are even more serious about competition, with four to six practices a week almost year-round. Their top competitive teams are usually joined by try-out or invitation only; a program like that is a major commitment for both you and your family.

CHAPTER 4

Meet the Competition

Many gymnasts choose to work out and improve their skills at their own gym just to get fit and have fun. This is called "recreational" or rec gymnastics, and it has all the advantages of a private gym: team-mates and friends, coaches and equipment, and ways to improve your physical fitness.

But testing yourself against other gymnasts—and against the standards set for each skill—is the best way

Going to gymnastics meets allows you to test your abilities against other teams. You can talk to other gymnasts and learn what they know.

to take it to the next level. No matter your age or skill level, there are options for you to track your improvement and test yourself at different gymnastics meets.

"Fun" Meets

Soon after starting, you'll be able do intra-gym fun meets, where everyone in your level at your gym takes turns doing the same routine on each apparatus: vault and floor for both boys and girls, uneven bars and balance beam for girls, and rings, parallel bars, pommel horse, and high bar for boys. You may also climb a rope or jump on the trampoline!

Your coaches will judge you on how well you perform skills for each event, and at the end you'll usually get a certificate or set of ribbons showing off how well you performed. At fun meets, you don't see your score or get ranked against other gymnasts.

Equipment for boys and girls tends to be different because boys often have more upper body strength and use their arms more.

Fun meets are sometimes held as part of bigger competitive meets involving kids from different gyms—as close to a competitive meet as it gets.

Xcel Meets

A newer competitive track is called Xcel, and it's organized and run by USA Gymnastics, just like top-level competitions. Xcel meets have it all: travel to other cities and gyms, real judges, real scores, ranked finishes, and podium awards. The competitive standards and skill groupings are more relaxed, though, so it's easier for families to fit it into busy schedules. There

ARTISTIC OR RHYTHMIC GYMNASTICS? WHICH IS WHICH?

When people think of gymnastics, they usually think of artistic gymnastics: vault, floor, bars. But there's another Olympic gymnastic sport: rhythmic gymnastics. Rhythmic routines are set to music. They value extreme flexibility, presentation, and style over power, height, and speed. It's performed on the same floor apparatus as artistic gymnastics, but ribbons, hoops, balls, and clubs are used as props to add drama and flair.

Rhythmic gymnastic routines are set to music and involve twirling ribbons. Rhythmic gymnastics allows you to show off your flexibility.

are also gyms that can prepare you to perform well at Xcel competitions.

Junior Olympics

The Junior Olympics program, maintained by USA Gymnastics, follows standards that are designed to prepare gymnasts for elite competition. To compete at these levels, it takes very frequent training and conditioning at a well-regarded competitive gym.

To compete in high school or college someday, this is the competitive track you should be on! And, like the name says, it's also the track you'll have to be on if you want a shot at the Olympics someday.

Very, very few gymnasts become Olympians. Even elite competitors who go on to make top college teams don't always get a chance to join the US National Team, let alone make the Olympic team.

But none of the Olympians you've seen on TV would have gotten there if they didn't start the way you're about to start now: by learning the basics, getting in shape and finding coaches and gyms that can make you better!

Words to Know

all-around How well a gymnast has performed on all events, measured by adding up individual scores on every event.

apparatus A piece of equipment used to do gymnastics routines.

coordination The ability to use different parts of your body together.

core Your stomach and back muscles.

event Part of a competition held on one apparatus.

flexibility How much your body and limbs are able to stretch.

meet An entire gymnastics competition, involving many different gyms, skill levels, and age groups.

momentum Speed in one direction.

podium Where top-scoring gymnasts stand to accept their awards after competition.

routine A memorized series of gymnastics skills performed on an apparatus, sometimes with music.

splits One of several different kinds of leg stretches that spread your legs wide apart.

Superman exercise A stomach and back exercise. Lay on the ground and raise your arms and legs so only your stomach is touching, then hold it as long as you can. Then roll over and do it on your back.

Learn More

Books

Hernandez, Laurie. *I Got This: To Gold and Beyond.* New York, NY: HarperCollins, 2017.

Kawa, Katie. *Sports Science: The Science of Gymnastics.* New York, NY: PowerKids Press, 2016.

Mason, Paul. *Sports Skills: Gymnastics.* New York, NY: Hachette Children's, 2018.

Websites

Active Kids
activekids.com/gymnastics
Find articles and stories about gymnastics, as well as resource locators for gyms and camps in your area.

Olympic.org
olympic.org/gymnastics-artistic
This is the International Olympic Committee's official home for artistic gymnastics.

USA Gymnastics
usagym.org/pages/find/gym.html
This USAG gym finder will help you find certified member gyms nearest to you.

Index